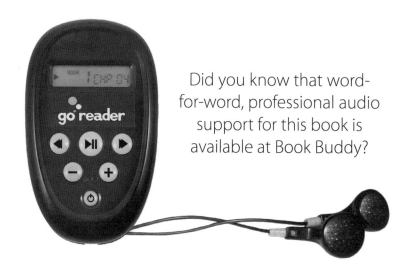

Did you know that word-for-word, professional audio support for this book is available at Book Buddy?

GoReader™ powered by Book Buddy is pre-loaded with word-for-word audio support to build strong readers and achieve Common Core standards.

The corresponding GoReader™ for this book can be found at: http://bookbuddyaudio.com

Or send an email to: info@bookbuddyaudio.com

YES SHE DID!

AEROSPACE

Yes She Did! Aerospace

Scobre Educational
2255 Calle Clara
La Jolla, CA 92037

Scobre Operations & Administration
42982 Osgood Road
Fremont, CA 94539

www.scobre.com
info@scobre.com

Scobre Educational publications may be purchased for educational, business, or sales promotional use.

Cover and layout design by Jana Ramsay
Copyedited by Renae Reed
Some photos by Getty Images

ISBN: 978-1-61570-940-3 (Soft Cover)
ISBN: 978-1-61570-939-7 (Library Bound)
ISBN: 978-1-61570-937-3 (eBook)

TABLE OF CONTENTS

CHAPTER 1
TAKING OFF

In 1903, the Wright brothers amazed the world by taking flight in the first working airplane. Suddenly, soaring with the birds was not only possible, it was about

FLYING HIGH

The Wright brothers fly their plane for the first time in Kitty Hawk, North Carolina.

6¢ AIR MAIL

WILBUR AND ORVILLE WRIGHT

FIRST FREE CONTROLLED AND SUSTAINED POWERED FLIGHT BY MAN

to become available to the common man. Fliers were no longer limited to slow,

DID YOU KNOW...

A patent office is where inventors apply for exclusive rights to their invention. If their application is approved, they have a "patent."

difficult-to-steer hot air balloons, or huge, expensive airships. Airplanes—which were small, quick, and could be built for only a few passengers—were the future of travel. The common man, however, was not alone in dreaming about flight. Many women, through their creativity and hard work, helped modern society take to the sky.

Elizabeth Lillian Todd, or Lillian as she liked to be called, was one of these groundbreaking women. At the turn of the century, it seemed like the whole world was reinventing itself with science and machinery. Todd was fascinated by the Wright brothers' achievement, and wanted to contribute to this brave new world of flight.

Todd was born in 1865 and grew up in Washington, D.C., where she inherited a love of mechanics from her grandfather. Her first job as a typewriter at the patent office fed her curiosity about technology and invention. In 1903, Lillian began doing her own research into aerodynamics, or the science behind flight. Her goal was to design and build her own airplane.

Over the next few years, Todd went to fairs and watched great airships floating in the sky. She went to the Metropolitan Museum in New York, where she studied the wing of a stuffed albatross, which is a kind of huge sea bird. She eventually based her own airplane's curved wings on the great bird. One of Todd's greatest concerns was improving the airplane's balance. To this end, she designed and patented a device, which had not been used in earlier models, to help with an airplane's balance.

When her airplane was finished, *The New York Times* was quick to point out that it was a woman's plane. The covers, which were made from heavy duty materi-al, were sewn "woman's fashion" rather than being fastened with tacks. The newspaper article clearly shows the mindset of many people in the early 1900s. They still viewed Todd's efforts as different than that of a man. However, they gave credit where credit was due, and also described Todd's creation as "one of the handsomest aeroplanes in existence."

Not only did Todd see flight as a fascinating wonder

BIG BIRD

Though they look similar, the albatross has a much longer wingspan than that of a seagull.

of human invention, she thought that airplanes could serve the country in a more practical way. After building her airplane, she donated it to the National Guard to help train pilots. She also started the Junior Aero Club, an organization that encouraged young people to become future pilots. Todd held meetings in her house, where the club members were surrounded by models

IN CONTROL

Amelia Earhart, at home behind the controls of her airplane.

of airplanes.

In Todd's day, women were just starting to become pilots themselves. Indeed, the Junior Aero Club members were boys, and Todd didn't actually fly her own airplane. The first U.S. woman pilot, Harriet Quimby, did not receive her license until 1911. However, Todd showed the world that flight and innovation are not only for men. Women, too, can defy gravity.

Though many people have followed in Lillian Todd's footsteps, there is one woman whose very name makes people think of flying. Ever since she was a little girl, Amelia Earhart was a thrill-seeker. Amelia's mother, also named Amelia, encouraged her daughters to run around the neighborhood, where they climbed trees and collected bugs. Amelia and her sister, Grace, even built a homemade "roller coaster" (a wooden box that flew down a ramp) after seeing a real one at the 1904 World's Fair. After

DID YOU KNOW...
Earhart saved up her own money to buy her airplane.

9

crashing down the ramp, Amelia told her sister that it felt like flying.

In 1920, Earhart went to an air show with her father, and took her first ride in an airplane. She later said, "By the time I had got two or three hundred feet off the ground, I knew I had to fly." By 1921, after a lot of hard work and hours in the cockpit, Earhart had earned her aviator pilot certificate.

Earhart wasn't content with simply flying—she wanted to be the best. In 1922, Earhart was the first woman to fly to an altitude of 14,000 feet above sea level. In 1928, Earhart became the first woman to fly across the Atlantic Ocean as a passenger. This experience was not satisfying to Earhart, who felt no more useful than "a sack of potatoes" during the flight. So, in 1932, Earhart tried to cross the Atlantic by herself.

The flight itself was very dangerous. Visibility was bad due to fog, her

DID YOU KNOW...

A female aviator is also called an aviatrix.

plane had a fuel leak, and her altitude gauge failed, which meant that Earhart could not tell how far above the ocean she was flying. When she finally landed in a sheep pasture in Ireland, Earhart became the first woman to fly across the Atlantic solo, and the first person to fly across the Atlantic twice. This flight wasn't just a grab for personal glory or attention. Earhart wanted to prove that in "jobs requiring intelligence, coordination, speed, coolness, and will-power," women were equal to men.

Indeed, while Earhart had many famous "firsts" during her career, she also

BREAKING RECORDS

Earhart smiles for the camera shortly after becoming the first woman to cross the Atlantic Ocean solo.

changed the face of aviation with her tireless efforts in support of women pilots. In 1929, Earhart founded the Women's Air Derby—a race from Santa Monica, California to Cleveland, Ohio, complete with a big cash prize. Earhart also helped start a professional organization for female pilots. This organization was called the Ninety-Nines because there were 99 founding members. The Ninety-Nines is still a great resource for women in aviation.

Sadly, Earhart is mostly remembered for her final flight. While attempting to become the first woman to circumnavigate, or fly around, the world, her airplane disappeared and was never found. The nation was stunned by this tragedy. Amelia Earhart was a beloved celebrity who captured the hearts of millions. To this day, she is probably the most famous pilot—man or woman—who ever lived.

DID YOU KNOW...

Though it has not yet been confirmed, many scientists believe that Earhart's plane crashed near Nikumaroro Island in the South Pacific.

CHAPTER 2
FLYING HIGHER

The early days of flight were full of challenges. Airplanes were dangerous, and many men and women lost their lives while aviation was still developing. However, some people faced the more basic challenge of simply being allowed to fly. Though the early 20th century was focused on the future of technology, in many ways society was still stuck in the past when it came to judging people

BREAKING BOUNDARIES

Bessie Coleman made history as the first African-American woman to earn a private pilot's license.

based on skin color. While Amelia Earhart was able to earn a U.S. pilot's license in 1921, Bessie Coleman was unable to do so because she was an African-American woman.

Coleman did not let this prejudice stop her. In 1920, after finding out that she could qualify for an aviation license in France, Coleman learned to speak French and traveled to Paris. On June 15, 1921, Bessie

THROUGH THE YEARS

Many pilots trained in France in the 1920s. Today, many people fly to Paris for a vacation.

Coleman became the first African-American woman to earn a pilot's license. Even after Coleman received her license, no one in the U.S. would give her additional lessons. Not discouraged, Coleman trained in Europe and returned to America as a stunt pilot. Stunt pilots use their planes to perform exciting tricks in the air.

Coleman, or "Queen Bess" as she was often called, was a media darling. Her shows were wildly popular. She was even offered a role in a movie, which she later turned down because she disapproved of the content. Tragically, at the height of her popularity in 1926, Coleman was a passenger in a fatal plane crash. Her death was a shock, and a reminder of the bravery of early aviators. They risked their lives every time they stepped in an airplane, but continued to pursue their dreams of flight.

Coleman's determination was an inspiration to

many people, including a woman named Willa Brown. In 1938, one year

after Amelia Earhart's plane vanished, Brown made history. She became the first African-American woman to earn a private pilot's license in the U.S. Brown and her husband, flight instructor Cornelius R. Coffey, wanted to improve opportunities for black pilots in the U.S. Together, they founded the Coffey School of Aeronautics in Illinois, and worked with the government to prepare African-American pilots for the military.

Before her death in 1992 at the age of 86, Brown broke many boundaries. She became the first African-American woman to hold a commercial U.S. pilot's license in addition to a private license, and the first African-American woman to become an officer in the Civil Air Patrol. During her lifetime, Brown worked tirelessly to prove that the bravery, determination, and intelligence needed to control an aircraft can arrive in

Many graduates of the Coffey School of Aeronautics went on to train at the Tuskegee Army Flying School. The Tuskegee Airmen fought in World War II, and became famous as the first African-American military aviators in the U.S. armed forces.

any gender or color.

The fight for flying equality was carried on by women like Beverly Burns. In 1974, Burns was a flight attendant for American Airlines when the words of one man changed her life. She was waiting between flights at an airport, chatting with a pilot. He told Burns why he thought there weren't many female commercial pilots: "Women are just not smart enough to do this

The Boeing 747 is one of the word's largest commercial airplanes.

job." Burns later described how his words affected her: "I knew as soon as the words came out of his mouth, 'women cannot be pilots,' that I wanted to be an airline captain immediately."

By the 1970s, flying by commercial airplane was becoming the norm. Though the demand for commercial airline pilots was rising, only a few of them were women. A 2013 study showed that only five percent of all commercial pilots in the U.S. and Canada were women. This number is

low for many reasons. Most commercial pilots come from a military background, but women were not allowed to fly fighter jets until 1993. In fact, American Airlines was the first major commercial airline to hire a woman pilot in 1973.

Burns fought, not only to prove one man wrong, but because she loved flying and wanted to rise to the top of her field. She earned her commertial pilot's license, and became one of the best. Among her accomplishments, Burns was the first woman to captain a Boeing 747 jumbo jet. Since a 747 can hold more than 400 passengers, during each flight Burns literally held hundreds of lives in her hands. When she retired in 2008, Burns had been a captain for 27 years, and clocked more than twenty-five thousand hours of flight time.

CHAPTER 3
BEYOND THE BLUE

After adventurers took to the skies, they decided to keep going and aim for the stars. Though humanity has dreamed of space travel for centuries, it wasn't until the 1960s that our technology finally caught up with our imaginations. In 1961, a Russian man named Lt. Yuri Gagarin was the first person launched into space. In 1969, Neil Armstrong spoke these famous words when he became the first person to set foot on the moon: "One small step for a man, one giant leap for mankind." In his speech, Armstrong used the word "mankind" to mean people in general, not just men. This is important to remember, because women, too,

DID YOU KNOW...

The first living creature launched into orbit was a Soviet dog named Laika, in 1957. Unfortunately, she did not survive the trip.

fought to travel beyond the limits of our world.

Geraldyn "Jerrie" Cobb was the first woman to pass all of the tests necessary to become an astronaut. Born in 1931, the daughter of a pilot, Cobb was a natural in the air. She earned her private pilot's license when she was just 17 years old, and her commercial license

MAN ON THE MOON

People have not been to the moon since 1972. However, the most recent unmanned trip to the moon was a Chinese lunar rover in 2013.

Peru is a large country on the coast of South America.

a year later. At age 21, though she was not in the military, Cobb helped transport military fighter planes from Miami to Columbia for the Peruvian Air Force. Being a woman, Cobb was not the transport company's first choice for the job. However, many male pilots were not willing to fly the dangerous trip over mountains and across the water. Cobb jumped at the chance to prove that she had the skill and bravery needed to do the job. Though things did not always go smoothly while flying to South America, Cobb was a success, and eventually became the chief pilot for the company's South American operations.

In 1959, the National Aeronautics and Space Administration (NASA)

was in the process of selecting astronauts for the Mercury space mission. Though they were not actually considering women for space flight at that time, they wanted to see how women would hold up to the difficult tests that every astronaut had to pass. When she was approached by NASA to take these tests, Cobb was a manager for Aero Design and Engineering Company, and had a record-setting career as a pilot. Among other awards, Cobb had received the Amelia Earhart Gold Medal of Achievement in 1949, and was named Pilot of the Year by the National Pilots Association in 1959. Cobb gladly volunteered to undergo NASA's testing, wanting to prove that women, like men, were fit for space travel.

Out of the 25 women selected for testing, Cobb was the only one who passed every round. She experienced physical and mental exams that pushed her beyond what most people can endure. For example, they tested Cobb's physical stamina by making her perform exercises, like riding a stationary bike, until she couldn't pedal anymore. A few of the stranger tests included electric shocks to check reflexes, ice water shots to the inner ear to find out how quickly a person could recover from being dizzy, and swallowing a three-foot rubber tube to test her stomach acid. They also had Cobb go through long periods of isolation, to see how she would hold up to the loneliness of being in space.

After passing all the exams, Cobb asked the government to let qualifying women train with men for space travel. However, at that time, NASA would only allow people who had military flight experience into their space program. In 1959, women were not allowed to fly in the military, and thus were not eligible for space travel. Many people thought that an exception should be

DID YOU KNOW...

Project Mercury was not named after the planet Mercury, but the Roman god known for speed.

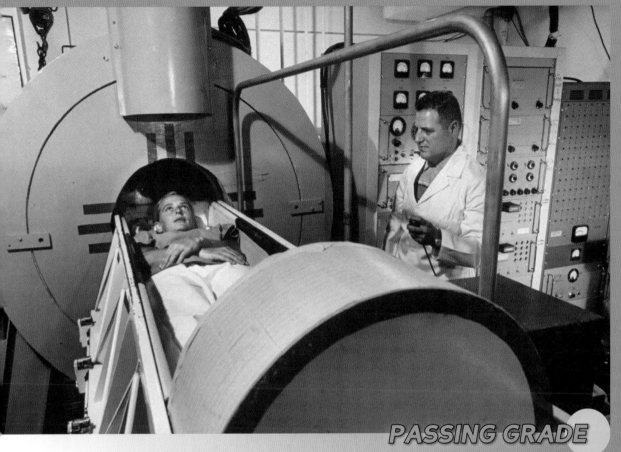

Jerrie Cobb had to take many physical exams to qualify for the astronaut program.

made for Cobb—whose 10,000 flight hours was more than double that of some qualifying male astronauts. Unfortunately, since those were not military hours, the government did not budge.

Jerrie Cobb never did travel into space, though such a journey always remained her dream. She continued to fly, and even won the Nobel Peace Prize in 1981 for flying medical supplies to struggling parts of the world, and for exploring new air routes.

Many women have benefited from Cobb's tireless efforts to promote equality in the space program. In 1983, Sally Ride became the first woman from the U.S. to travel into space. Growing up, Ride's parents encouraged her and her sister to pursue anything they were interested in, even if those interests weren't typically for girls. In an interview, Ride's mother said that she and her husband "simply forgot to tell them that there were things they couldn't do." As a child, Ride was always the best at sports, beating other kids, boys and girls, at football and baseball. As she got older, Ride balanced athletics with academics. She was a tennis champion, and earned a PhD in physics from Stanford University.

In 1978, Ride saw an ad in the Stanford newspaper for the NASA Space Program. Ride jumped at the chance to become an astronaut. Like Cobb before her,

Ride passed all of NASA's tests. After a year-long training program, Ride became eligible for space travel.

Before becoming the first American woman in space, Ride worked for NASA for several years. Among other accomplishments, Ride helped NASA develop a robotic arm for the space shuttle. When NASA announced that Ride would be the first American woman to travel into space, many people in the media questioned how a woman would handle such stressful conditions. During an interview before the launch, some people even asked Ride if she would cry if something went wrong.

PRACTICE MAKES PERFECT

Sally Ride completes some final training exercises before her first NASA mission in 1983.

Ride patiently answered their rude questions, saying that she did not think of herself as a woman who was about to make history, but as an astronaut doing her job.

During her career as an astronaut, Ride went on two successful launches on the space shuttle Challenger, first in 1983, then in 1984. She was not just along for the ride, but

READY TO LAUNCH

Sally Ride floats inside the Challenger in 1984.

was an important member of the crew. For example, one of her duties was operating the robotic arm that she had helped design. She was the first woman to retrieve a satellite with a robotic arm.

In her lifetime, Ride was inducted into the Astronaut Hall of Fame, the National Women's Hall of Fame, and was twice awarded the NASA Space Flight Medal. Ride always said that she owed a great debt to the women who came before her, who had fought so hard for equality.

To help future generations, Ride developed educational programs that encouraged children, particularly girls, to learn about science. After her death in 2012, Sally Ride was given the Space Foundations' highest possible honor: the General James E. Hill Lifetime Space Achievement Award.

CHAPTER 4
TAKING CHARGE

In the years following Sally Ride's historic trip into space, women started to not only serve as key members of the space program, but to also fill important leadership roles. In 1999, for example, Eileen Collins became the first woman to command a space shuttle.

Born in 1956, Collins was a teenager when the U.S. began sending people to the moon. Growing up, space travel was not just a dream in her world, but a reality. Early on, Collins set her sights on becoming a pilot and an astronaut. However, when she began to pursue her dream, women from the U.S. had still never been to space. Collins knew she would have to work

DID YOU KNOW...

Eileen Collins' parents are immigrants from Ireland. In 2006, Collins was recognized with an honorary doctor of science degree from the National University of Ireland.

extremely hard to succeed in a career path that was still largely uncharted for women. To that end, Collins studied math and science in school, and eventually earned master's degrees in both operations research and space systems management.

Before her acceptance into the astronaut program in 1990, Collins met one of NASA's requirements by earning her pilot's license. First, she trained at the world-class Vance Air Force Base in Oklahoma. Collins then enrolled in the U.S. Air Force Test Pilot School— the second woman to ever attend this program. She later put her pilot training to good use, becoming the first woman to pilot a space

LARGER THAN LIFE

Eileen Collins stands next to a model space shuttle after being selected for astronaut training in 1990.

Collins talks to the media before her 2005 Discovery mission.

shuttle in 1995.

Though Collins made history in 1999 as the first female shuttle commander, it was her final mission in 2005 that truly proved her capacity to lead. Two years earlier, there had been a horrible accident that shook the foundations of the space program. On February 1, 2003, the space shuttle Columbia was damaged during take-off, and later broke apart when it reentered the earth's atmosphere. All of the crew members were killed. This tragedy derailed the space program for several years, as NASA worked to improve safety, and make sure a disaster like this would never happen again.

In 2005, when Collins took command of the space shuttle Discovery, the main goal was to bring supplies to the International Space Station (ISS). However, NASA also wanted to use the Discovery mission to restore the country's faith in space travel. When the Discovery was also damaged during the launch, some people worried that there would be another tragic ending.

To make sure the shuttle would return home in one piece, the Discovery had to be repaired while still in space. As part of the repair process, Collins became the first person, male or female, to fly a space shuttle in a complete 360-degree pitch maneuver. This meant that the shuttle turned all the way around,

DID YOU KNOW...

The International Space Station (ISS) is a research laboratory in orbit around Earth. People from many different countries live and work on the ISS.

so people on the ISS could take pictures of all sides of the shuttle. In this way, they were able to identify, and repair, all of the damage. Almost 14 days after take-off, Collins and her crew returned to earth, safe and sound. When Collins announced her retirement a year later, NASA chief Michael Griffin said, "Eileen Collins is a living, breathing example of the best that our nation has to offer."

Many other women have risen through the ranks to become leaders in NASA. In 2013, former astronaut Ellen Ochoa was named director of Johnson Space Center (JSC). First opened in 1963, JSC became the hub of human spaceflight training. This facility is also the home of mission control, where NASA communicates with space shuttles in flight. When an Apollo 13 astronaut famously spoke the words, "Houston, we've had a problem," he was speaking to someone at JSC.

Ochoa is the second woman to serve as director of this historic facility, and the first of Hispanic descent. Like Eileen Collins before her, Ochoa began to dream of space travel before Sally Ride had broken that particular barrier for U.S. women. In fact, Ochoa was already studying for her PhD in electrical engineering at Stanford University when Sally Ride, a fellow Stanford grad, went on her first space mission.

Though all astronauts are adventurers and ex-plorers, they are also scientists at heart. Before becoming an astronaut herself, Ochoa was a research engineer. She

JET-SETTING
Astronaut Ellen Ochoa trains at the Vance Air Force Base while preparing for a 1993 space mission.

SUNSCREEN

The Earth's ozone layer helps protect our world from the sun's harsh rays.

devoted her life to improving technology for the space program. One of her many inventions was a device that could scan objects for damage or defects—improving astronaut safety. Ochoa began to hone her leadership skills while overseeing 35 research scientists at NASA's Intelligent Systems Technology Branch in California.

In 1990, NASA accepted Ochoa into the space program in recognition of her many contributions to the space industry. During her first space mission in 1993,

Ochoa helped collect information about damage to the Earth's ozone layer. This trip also marked Ochoa as the first Hispanic woman in space. After four missions, and nine years as an active astronaut, Ochoa logged almost 1,000 hours (41 days) in space. When Ochoa took over as director of JSC, her promotion was not lightly given. She had already proved her ability to lead while serving as the deputy director of JSC since 2007.

During her long career, Ochoa has been honored with many awards, including the Hispanic Engineer Albert Baez Award for Outstanding Technical Contribution to Humanity, and NASA's Women in Aerospace Outstanding Achievement Award.

One of her many goals in life is to promote science education among students. When not overseeing the 3,200 people who work for JSC, Ochoa gives speeches around the county, inspiring future scientists and astronauts.

DID YOU KNOW...

Two schools—one in Pasco, Washington and one in Cudahy, California—have been named after Ellen Ochoa.

CHAPTER 5
THE FUTURE OF FLIGHT

Flight was once the cutting edge of adventure and invention. Early women pilots, such as Amelia Earhart and Bessie Coleman, were seen as death-defying daredevils and—to many people—heroes. In modern times, flying across the country has become much safer, and even routine. Though male commercial pilots still outnumber their female peers, passengers no longer think twice when a woman's voice announces, "This is your captain speaking."

Even space exploration is becoming accessible to the masses, by way of the internet. In 2013, astronaut Karen Nyberg sent a YouTube video from the ISS, demonstrating how to wash your hair in zero gravity with a bag of warm water and no-rinse shampoo. In the video, Nyberg's long, blond hair stood straight up, and she caught water droplets that floated away from her head.

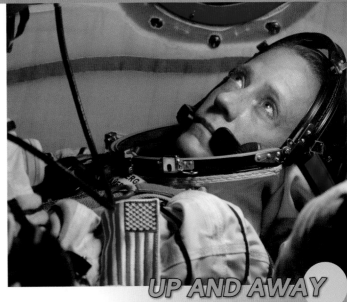

UP AND AWAY

Karen Nyberg trains in a space capsule before a trip to the ISS.

However, there are still new horizons to cross, and new technology to advance. Alexandra Loubeau, a NASA aerospace engineer, is researching how to lower the noise a plane makes when it breaks the sound barrier. This sound is called a "sonic boom," and can hurt people's ears and frighten animals. Loubeau is trying to reduce this noise, so that commercial airplanes can fly at supersonic speeds without causing a disturbance.

Women are also helping plan humanity's first manned trip to Mars. A non-profit organization called Mars One is aiming to send people on a one-way mission

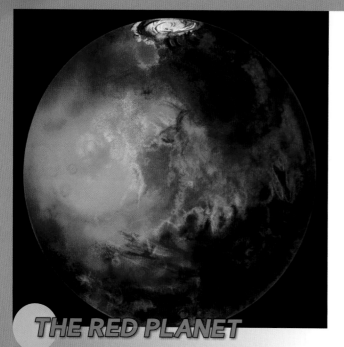

THE RED PLANET

Mars, sometimes visible in the night sky, is a bright red color. This planet was named after the Roman god of war.

to the red planet. Suzanne Flinkenflögel is Mars One's director of communications. Flinkenflögel, who worked in both Spain and Mexico before joining Netherlands-based Mars One, encourages people around the world to apply for the program. According to a 2014 Huffingtonpost.com article, 472 women have already advanced past Mars One's first selection round for the mission to Mars.

Though no one is heading to Mars right now (Mars One's current timeline has the first mission launching in 2024), there is no saying how far women may one day travel. For scientists, explorers and thrill-seekers, not even the sky is the limit.

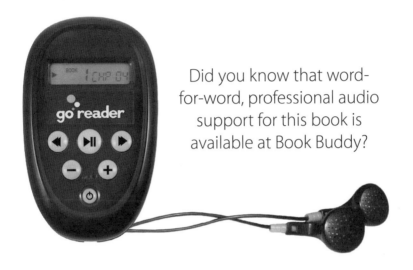

Did you know that word-
for-word, professional audio
support for this book is
available at Book Buddy?

GoReader™ powered by Book Buddy is pre-loaded with word-for-word audio
support to build strong readers and achieve Common Core standards.

The corresponding GoReader™ for this book can
be found at: http://bookbuddyaudio.com

Or send an email to: info@bookbuddyaudio.com